# STEVEN SPIELBERG

### By Geoffrey M. Horn

**WORLD ALMANAC® LIBRARY**

**Please visit our web site at:  www.worldalmanaclibrary.com**
**For a free color catalog describing World Almanac® Library's list**
**of high-quality books and multimedia programs, call 1-800-848-2928 (USA)**
**or 1-800-387-3178 (Canada).  World Almanac® Library's fax:  (414) 332-3567.**

**Library of Congress Cataloging-in-Publication Data**

Horn, Geoffrey M.
    Steven Spielberg / by Geoffrey M. Horn.
       p. cm. — (Trailblazers of the modern world)
    Includes bibliographical references and index.
    Summary: Discusses the personal life and professional career of the successful motion picture
producer and director, Steven Spielberg.
    ISBN 0-8368-5080-7 (lib. bdg.)
    ISBN 0-8368-5240-0 (softcover)
    1. Spielberg, Steven, 1947—Juvenile literature.  2. Motion picture producers and directors—
United States—Biography—Juvenile literature.  [1. Spielberg, Steven, 1947-.  2. Motion picture
producers and directors.]  I. Title.  II. Series.
PN1998.3.S65H67   2002
791.43'0233'092—dc21
[B]                                       2002069141

This edition first published in 2002 by
**World Almanac® Library**
330 West Olive Street, Suite 100
Milwaukee, WI  53212  USA

This edition © 2002 by World Almanac® Library.

Project editor: Mark J. Sachner
Design and page production: Scott M. Krall
Photo research: Diane Laska-Swanke
Editor: Betsy Rasmussen
Indexer: Walter Kronenberg
Production direction: Susan Ashley

Photo credits: Arnold Spielberg Courtesy of Getty Images: 10; © Bettmann/CORBIS: 6, 15; Courtesy of Dale Dye/Getty
Images: 8; Courtesy of Getty Images: cover; Dirck Halstead/Getty Images: 38 bottom; Fotos Int'l Courtesy of Getty
Images: 7, 18 bottom, 26, 31; George DeSota/Getty Images: 38 top; Getty Images: 9, 14, 37 bottom; Hulton
Archive/Getty Images: 32 top, 36 bottom, 40 bottom right; © Kim Kulish/CORBIS Sygma: 5; Marc Rylewski/Getty
Images: 32 bottom; Paramount Courtesy of Getty Images: 12; Photofest: 13, 16, 18 top, 19, 20, 21, 22, 24, 27 both,
28 both, 30, 34 both, 35 both, 37 top, 39 both, 40 top & bottom left, 42, 43 both; Universal Courtesy of Getty Images:
4, 23, 36 top; © Walt Disney: 25

Printed in the United States of America

1 2 3 4 5 6 7 8 9 06 05 04 03 02

Words that appear in the glossary are printed in **boldface**
type the first time they occur in the text.

# CHAPTER 1

# MASTER ENTERTAINER

Ads showing this terrifying image of a killer shark helped turn *Jaws* into the first summer blockbuster.

The film world changed forever on June 20, 1975. That is the day *Jaws*—a scary movie about a killer shark—opened nationwide in more than 450 theaters. *Jaws* was a huge hit and the first summer blockbuster. It also launched Steven Spielberg on a career that has made him the wealthiest and most powerful filmmaker in Hollywood history.

Spielberg knew from the first screams at the earliest sneak previews in March that he had a hit on his hands. Universal, the **studio** that financed the film, left nothing to chance, however. For the first time ever, Universal bought ads on national television to promote the film. The *Jaws* logo—upward thrusting snout, gaping mouth, huge teeth, innocent swimmer above—showed up on beach towels, T-shirts, pool toys, even the cover of *Time* magazine.

For their daring and confidence, Spielberg and the studio were well rewarded. The film cost about $12 million to make, and Universal spent about $1.8 million advertising the movie before it opened. Within two weeks, *Jaws* earned back every dollar it cost to produce. The film went on to break box-office records. It was the first motion picture to pass the $100 million mark in ticket sales.

Ticket prices now are higher than they were in 1975, and today's blockbusters routinely open on two thousand screens or more. Even so, *Jaws* still ranks among the top thirty most successful films ever made. Worldwide, the film has earned more than $470 million, including $260 million in the United States and over $210 million abroad. That is only the money the film has made from theater ticket sales. It does not include revenues from TV broadcasts, videocassette and DVD sales and rentals, and sales of posters and other items.

## ENVYING HIS SUCCESS

Today, Spielberg commands a personal fortune worth more than $2 billion. Since 1975, moviegoers throughout the world have paid more than $5 billion to see his films. In addition to directing his own movies, Spielberg is a cofounder and top executive of one of Hollywood's biggest entertainment firms, DreamWorks SKG. He owns homes in Pacific Palisades, California, and in East Hampton, New York, on the eastern tip of Long Island. What does he do with all that wealth? Here is a recent example. As a gift for his wife, actress Kate Capshaw, who loves horses, he called in a design team to build stables and a 24,000-square-foot (2,230-square-meter) outdoor riding ring in the Sullivan Canyon area of Los Angeles.

For a long time, many people in the film world were jealous of Spielberg's wealth and talent. Other excellent **directors** had to struggle to get money to make their films. These directors made serious movies that were sometimes difficult to watch—films that set out to challenge audiences with compli-

Spielberg launched DreamWorks SKG in 1994 with David Geffen (left) and Jeffrey Katzenberg (right).

cated ideas and complex emotions. Spielberg, on the other hand, made audiences laugh, cry, and scream— and love every minute of it. He churned out blockbuster after blockbuster and was a multimillionaire before he turned thirty. Somehow, it all seemed too easy. Sure, Spielberg was popular, but was he really that good?

The belief that Spielberg had come too far too fast helps explain how few major awards he won during the 1970s and 1980s. *Jaws* was nominated for an **Academy Award** as Best Picture of 1975 but did not win. Spielberg was nominated for directing *Close Encounters of the Third Kind* (1977) and *Raiders of the Lost Ark* (1981), but he did not win for those films, either. *E.T. the Extra-Terrestrial* (1982), which many now regard as a classic, was nominated for both Best Picture and Best Director. It lost twice to *Gandhi*—a film admired when it came out but seldom watched today.

In the Academy's balloting for *The Color Purple* (1985), the film world's message was clear. The film was up for eleven **Oscars**—but it did not win any. In the directing category, Spielberg was not even nominated.

Spielberg learned a lot about filmmaking from watching the movies of Alfred Hitchcock. Like *Jaws,* Hitchcock's *The Birds* (1963) tells a scary story about the conflict between people and nature.

### Oscar Snubs

Steven Spielberg was not the first and certainly will not be the last director to be snubbed at Oscar time. One director often overlooked by the Academy was Alfred Hitchcock, a great master of movie suspense and an important influence on Spielberg. Hitchcock, the director of *Rear Window* (1954) and *Psycho* (1960), never won an Oscar for directing. He was nearing the end of his career when he was presented with the Irving G. Thalberg Award for 1967.

Children often have very important roles in Spielberg's films. Here, the director gives actor Henry Thomas some pointers for a scene in *E.T.*

Spielberg, the most popular director of his time, was not personally honored by the Academy until March 1987, when he received the Irving G. Thalberg Memorial Award—which is given for work as a **producer**. His acceptance speech to the members of the Academy signaled that he knew he had a long way to go to earn their respect. "I'm proud to have my name on this award," he said, "because it reminds me of how much growth as an artist I have ahead of me in order to be worthy of standing in the company of those who have received this before me."

## Movie Facts

Total annual U.S. box-office receipts: **$8.4 billion**
Number of tickets sold each year in the United States: **about 1.5 billion**
Average cost of a ticket: **$5.66**
Number of films released in the United States in a single year: **482**
Average cost of making a feature film:
    **$47.7 million (up from $9.4 million in 1980)**
Average cost of marketing the movie:
    **$31 million (up from $4.3 million in 1980)**
Number of U.S. movie screens:
    **36,764 (up from 17,590 in 1980)**
Number of U.S. households with a VCR: **96.2 million**
DVD players shipped to U.S. dealers: **12.7 million**
Titles available on DVD: **13,000 (up from 600 in 1997)**

Source: Motion Picture Association of America.
All figures are for 2001 unless otherwise noted.

Spielberg instructs the cast and crew of *Saving Private Ryan*, one of his many movies with a World War II setting.

## EARNING RESPECT

It is not hard to spot the themes that run through Spielberg's films: The conflict of good versus evil, especially during **World War II**; the power of hope in the darkest times; the relationship, often destructive, between people and nature; the value of family; the importance of childhood—and of kindness to children.

The director's challenge in the 1990s was to take these themes, which he had used again and again as a young filmmaker, and revisit them in a more mature way. This was especially true of the war theme, which forms the backdrop for *Raiders of the Lost Ark* and numerous other Spielberg films. In *Raiders*, the **Nazis**—the enemies of the United States in World War II—were almost cartoon characters. In *Schindler's List* (1993), however, the Nazis, and the ugly ideas they stood for, became frighteningly real.

Similarly, in *Raiders*, the war mostly served as a setting for the thrilling but unlikely exploits of the hero, Indiana Jones. In *Saving Private Ryan* (1998), however, the director gave his audience a much more honest view of war. His goal was to show people what it really felt like to be at the center of the battle for Europe during World War II.

To Spielberg's surprise, audiences were willing to follow him on his journey into adulthood. Both *Schindler's List* and *Saving Private Ryan* were commercially successful. In fact, despite its harshness, *Ryan* became one of Spielberg's most popular works.

In the film world, these two movies also served an important purpose. They finally earned Spielberg the respect he craved. He won his first Oscar as director for *Schindler* in 1994 and his second for *Ryan* in 1999. *Schindler* was also the first of his films to win an Academy Award as Best Picture.

As a head of his own studio and one of the richest men in the United States, Spielberg has the freedom to make almost any film he wants. How he uses that freedom—and develops his art—may shape the history of movies for decades to come.

Success at the 1994 Oscars earned the director a kiss from his wife, actress Kate Capshaw (right), and the admiration of his mother, Leah.

# CHAPTER 2

# BOY WITH A CAMERA

Steven Allan Spielberg was born in the Jewish Hospital of Cincinnati, Ohio, on December 18, 1946. The year of his birth has been the subject of some dispute, and some books still say he was born in 1947. Spielberg himself is partly responsible for the confusion. The boyish-looking director sometimes pretended to be younger than he was when he thought that might help his career.

His mother, originally Leah Posner, was trained as a concert pianist. She put her musical career on hold when she married Arnold Spielberg in 1945, but she never lost her love for music. From her, Steven seems to have inherited his artistic leanings, along with the sure-handed sense of rhythm that drives his films.

Steven had a stormy childhood, and he did not make life easy for his three younger sisters. He always had a vivid imagination and would tease his sisters in creative ways. Once, he cut the head off a sister's favorite doll and presented it to her on a platter, garnished with lettuce and tomato. Another cruel trick involved locking his sisters in a closet. "I remember a movie on television with a Martian who kept a severed head in a fishbowl," he recalled. "So I locked them in a closet with a fishbowl. I can still hear the terror breaking in their voices."

"When he was growing up, I didn't know he was a genius," his mother told an interviewer. "Frankly, I didn't know what the hell he was. You see, Steven wasn't exactly cuddly.

This photo shows Steven as a baby, with his father and mother. She later described her son as more scary than cuddly in his boyhood days.

What he was was scary. . . . His badness was so original that there weren't even books to tell you what to do."

FATHER AND SON

Steven's father, Arnold Spielberg, a radio operator, served with an air squadron that blew up Japanese bridges and rail lines in Burma during World War II. After the war, he earned a degree in electronics from the University of Cincinnati. He went on to become a pioneer in the development of electronic computers. He worked hard and did not have as much time to spend with his son as Steven would have liked. Arnold's difficult work schedule did not help his and Leah's marriage, either.

## Film Focus: Getting Started

Spielberg was asked in a 1974 interview what advice he would give to a young person just starting out.

*Do a lot of writing, try to make a short film or two, cut it yourself, also do the photography, and if you're a ham, star in it. It's almost impossible to get work with none of your abilities showing. Studios aren't buying qualities like eagerness and enthusiasm and a willingness to learn. They want material evidence that you're a movie-maker who's going to turn a profit. They want to see and feel how good you are. . . .*

*I began by making 8 and 16mm films, some for $15 apiece and some for $200. You can't excuse yourself by saying, "Well, I can't raise the money to make the short film to get into the front door and show my work." It's not expensive to make little movies, even if they're . . . done with a . . . camera you've borrowed from a friend.*

The older Spielberg wanted his son to become an engineer, but Steven had little talent for science. Still, he shared with his father an interest in new technology—an interest aided by the fact that his uncle Irvin, also an engineer, worked for the U.S. space program. Steven also shared with his father a love for science fiction. Arnold read every science fiction magazine he could get his hands on, and his son did, too.

Arnold Spielberg had one other interest he passed on to his son. He liked to make movies. Leah had bought him an 8mm camera, which Arnold used to make home movies of family camping trips. Steven thought his father's films were boring and was sure he could do better. "I'd take the camera and kind of heighten the reality of the field trip," he told a reporter in 1978. "I'd make my parents let me out of the car so I could run up ahead 200 yards. Then I'd wave them forward and they'd pull up and get out of the car and start unpacking. I began to actually stage the camping trips and cut the bad footage out."

Scenes like this one from *The Greatest Show on Earth* inspired Steven to make his first real film in 1957.

## FIRST FILMS

The Spielbergs moved to New Jersey in 1949 after Arnold got his college degree and was hired by RCA to help develop its first computer. During the next seven years, all three of Steven's sisters were born: Anne (who became a screenwriter and producer) in 1949, Susan in 1953, and Nancy in 1956.

While the family was living in New Jersey, Arnold took his five-year-old son to a movie theater for the first time. The film was Cecil B.

DeMille's circus epic, *The Greatest Show on Earth* (1952). Steven was not thrilled by the movie—he was expecting to see a real circus—but he was impressed by one scene in the film that showed a terrible train wreck.

By the time he was eight years old, Steven was putting on puppet shows in the basement of the family home. He also staged elaborate battle scenes, using plastic and rubber toy soldiers and ketchup for blood. It was not until after the family moved in 1957 to the Arcadia section of Phoenix, Arizona, where his father took a job with General Electric, that Steven began making his own movies.

For his first real film, the three-minute *The Last Train Wreck* (1957), Steven borrowed a page from the Cecil B. DeMille playbook. The whole film was based on his toy electric trains crashing into each other. He cut back and forth from shots of a train going from right to left to shots of a train going from left to right. He then built suspense with "reaction shots" of plastic figures looking on in horror. When the film was developed and projected on a screen, the young director was amazed at how, when shot close up, his little engines looked like huge locomotives.

From his earliest days as a filmmaker to more recent works like *Amistad,* Spielberg has understood the importance of film editing.

## RISING IN PHOENIX

As Spielberg entered his teen years, his films grew longer and more ambitious. *The Last Gunfight* (1958) ran nine minutes, *Fighter Squad* (1959–1960) ran fifteen, and *Escape to Nowhere* (1959–1962), which won first prize at an amateur film festival, ran forty. For a battle scene in *Escape to Nowhere*, he had six cameras going at the same time, all filming from different angles. Instead of gun-

A skyline view of Phoenix, Arizona, in the early 1960s.

powder, he used flour to show what looked like shells blowing up. Later, he explained how the effect worked: "I dug two holes in the ground and put a balancing board loaded with flour between them, then covered it with a bush. When a 'soldier' ran over it, the flour made a perfect geyser in the air."

Encouraged by his parents, Steven found movies a perfect way to express his creativity. Filmmaking also served another purpose. When he first came to Arizona, he felt like an outsider—a skinny, geeky Jewish kid with a New Jersey accent. Making movies helped him gain acceptance. He joined the Boy Scouts and used his film skills to earn a merit badge in photography. Like his father, Steven was a very good storyteller, and he loved to scare his fellow Scouts by telling ghost stories around the campfire. He could reward his school friends and boss around bullies by giving them parts in his films.

Steven did not date much in high school, and he probably did not realize how much some girls liked him. "Some of my friends had major crushes on him," his sister Anne recalled. "If you looked at a picture of him then, you'd say, 'Yes, there's a nerd. There's the crewcut, the flattop. There are the

## Film Focus: Editing the Movie

*The Last Train Wreck* was "edited in the camera"— that means the ten-year-old filmmaker took shot after shot in exactly the order they appear in the finished film. Later, he discovered a better way to edit his movies.

*I edited everything myself. Once I discovered how important the cut was, I never cut in the camera again. I would shoot all the master shots on one roll, all the closeups on another roll and all the action and trick shots on a third roll. Then I would break the film down and hang the separate shots on pins on a little makeshift cutting rack in my bedroom at home. I'd label each one with a piece of tape, identifying it by number, what was in the scene, and where it was to go. Then I would pull each one off its pin and cut the way they cut today. So I really assembled the film. I became a film editor before I became a professional director.*

Some young filmmakers still use methods like those Spielberg described in 1978. Student films can also be turned into video files and edited on a computer. Whatever the technique, good editing is still crucial to making a good film.

ears. There's the skinny body.' But he really had an incredible personality. He could make people do things. He made everything he was going to do sound like you wished you were a part of it."

The high point of Steven's Phoenix years came on March 24, 1964, when a downtown theater premiered *Firelight*, his first feature-length movie. The sci-fi film ran nearly two and one-half hours and had sound, music, **dialogue**, and ingenious visual effects. The whole thing cost only about $400, according to Spielberg. He charged five hundred people a dollar a ticket and made a $100 profit, he told an interviewer in 1978.

Arnold put up the money for the production and helped in the projection booth. Leah let Steven use the whole house as his studio. All three sisters worked on the film, and the youngest, Nancy, had a starring role as a young girl kidnapped by space aliens.

The period of family togetherness did not last long. The day after the Phoenix premiere, the Spielbergs left Arizona for California, where Arnold landed a new, high-pressure computer job with IBM. Each day he worked from seven-thirty in the morning until seven or eight o'clock at night. His brutal work schedule took its toll on his relationships with his children and Leah. By 1965, their marriage had fallen apart, and Arnold had moved into his own apartment. The following year, Arnold and Leah Spielberg were divorced.

Steven had been somebody in Phoenix. Now, in California, he was just the oldest child of divorced parents. He needed to get an education, make some money, and—most of all—break into the film business in a big way. It took him nearly five years to do it, and they felt like the longest years of his life.

The traditional way to edit a Hollywood movie was to run strips of film through a machine like this one. Today, many professional filmmakers edit their work on a computer.

# CHAPTER 3

# BREAKTHROUGH

Spielberg's own production company, Amblin Entertainment, is named for the short film that gave him his big break in the movie business. Amblin's logo is based on the famous flying bicycle scene from *E.T.*

Uprooted from Phoenix, Spielberg spent a wretched senior year at Saratoga High School, not far from San Jose. His parents were splitting up, and bullying by bigger classmates made his life even more miserable. "Suddenly, in this **affluent**, three-cars-to-one-household suburb, these big, macho guys made an event out of my being Jewish." Decades later, he could still remember the hurt he felt, both physical and emotional. "They beat me up regularly after school. I took some pretty good shots. Finally, my parents had to pick me up in a car, which was humiliating in itself because we lived close enough for me to walk home."

His college prospects were not too good. He applied to the state's two top film schools, at the University of Southern California and the University of California at Los Angeles. Both USC and UCLA turned him down because of his weak high school grades. Instead, he went to California State University at Long Beach. He already knew more about making films than any of the professors.

Most of Spielberg's real education during this period came at Universal Studios, where he had begun hanging out in the summer of 1964. He did office work, ran errands, and learned as much as he could about how a major Hollywood company handled all the details of film and TV production. "I visited every set I could, got to know people, observed techniques, and just generally absorbed the atmosphere," he said. His grand plan, he told Universal's film librarian, Chuck Silvers, was to become a professional director before he reached twenty-one. He missed the mark by only a few months.

Spielberg understood that he had to do more than show the studio heads that he could make really good films. He also had to show his bosses that he could make films that would make money. To demonstrate his abilities, he raised about $20,000 in 1968 and made a short movie called *Amblin'*. This twenty-six-minute film told the story of two young hitchhikers who fall in and out of love. It had no dialogue, but it did have music and was beautifully photographed. Spielberg showed the film to

## Film Focus: Camera Angles

There is a show-off-like feeling to some of Spielberg's early work, which the director later admitted.

*When I was first starting out, I used a lot of fancy shots. Some of the compositions were very nice, but I'd usually be shooting through somebody's armpit or angling past someone's nose. I got a lot of that out of my system and became less preoccupied with mechanics and began to search more for the literary quality in the scripts I was reading.*

Allen Daviau, who first collaborated with Spielberg on *Amblin'*, won acclaim for his work on *Empire of the Sun* (above).

Gertie (played by Drew Barrymore) kisses her extraterrestrial friend in *E.T.*

Chuck Silvers, who immediately contacted Sidney Sheinberg, production chief for Universal's television division. By early December—shortly before his twenty-second birthday—Spielberg was the youngest director on the Universal payroll.

*Amblin'* was an important film for Spielberg—and not just because it earned him his first professional contract. It proved that he could use camera movement, lighting, scenery, and sound to convey powerful emotions, even when the characters did not speak a single word. Spielberg worked on the movie with Allen Daviau, who served as **cinematographer**—the person directly responsible for deciding how a particular scene should be lit and photographed. Daviau later received Oscar nominations for cinematography on such Spielberg films as *E.T.*, *The Color Purple*, and *Empire of the Sun*. When Spielberg founded his own production company in 1984, he named it Amblin Entertainment after the film that got him his first full-time job.

### ADVENTURES ON THE SMALL SCREEN

Although Spielberg continued to hunger for big screen success, his contract called for him to direct programs for television. On his very first television job, the "Eyes" episode of *Night Gallery*, the young man was given the task of directing Joan Crawford, a woman who had more than forty years of acting experience and was already a Hollywood legend. The shoot lasted several days, and Spielberg later admitted he spent the whole time frightened out of his wits but trying not to show it. Crawford did as much as she could to put the first-time director at ease. When she died in 1977 at the age of seventy-two, Spielberg said these words at her funeral: "She treated me like I knew what I was doing, and I didn't. I loved her for that."

Spielberg went on to direct several made-for-TV movies. One of his major successes was "Murder by the Book" (1971). This was an early episode of the *Columbo* mystery series, which starred Peter Falk as the clever detective in a rumpled raincoat. The cinematographer on the episode was Russell Metty, a crusty veteran who had won an Oscar a decade earlier. "He's a kid!" Metty groused. "Does he get a milk and cookie break?" Despite Metty's complaints, the show was expertly shot and has been reissued on home video.

Spielberg's most impressive 1971 effort was *Duel*. This made-for-TV movie was later released in theaters. Shot in little more than two weeks—at a cost, Spielberg claimed, of only $425,000—*Duel* shows a high-tension battle between an ordinary businessman (played by Dennis Weaver) and a killer truck. What makes this extreme portrait of road rage so terrifying is that the

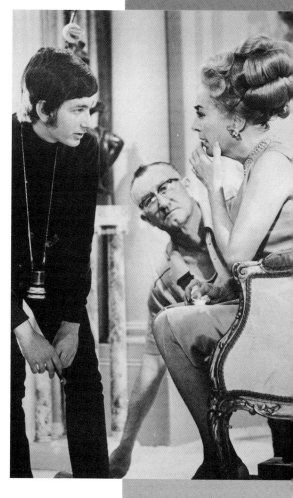

The "Eyes" episode of *Night Gallery* matched the inexperienced Spielberg with a Hollywood legend, Joan Crawford.

camera never gives us or Weaver a clear view of the truck driver who is out to get him. Like every great horror film director, Spielberg learned that what we do not see can be even more scary than what we do see.

The response to *Duel* was so positive that Universal offered him the chance to direct his first full-fledged theatrical film, *The Sugarland Express* (1974). Two things make this movie memorable. The first is a touching performance by Goldie Hawn as a woman who persuades her husband to escape from prison so they can be reunited with their baby. The second is the car stunts—lots of them—each more exciting than the last.

Audiences were not wild about the film, but many movie critics were. "In terms of the pleasure that technical assurance gives an audience, this film is one of the most phenomenal **debut** films in the history of movies," said the hard-to-please Pauline Kael, who called Spielberg "one of those wizard directors who can make trash entertaining."

# Film Focus: Spectacular Stunts

In a 1974 interview, Spielberg explained how he pulled off sensational car stunts in *The Sugarland Express*.

*There is an individual, personal excitement on the part of every stunt man to beat the other stunt guy. And when you get six highly competitive stunt drivers in one scene, wonderful things can happen before the camera. An example of this is the scramble of cars from the football stadium when Captain Tanner gets word there's a shoot-out in progress at a used car lot only a mile away. We had eleven stunt drivers that day from Hollywood and Chicago, and we had over forty-five actual police officers from Texas. A directive had come down from the Department of Public Safety to all their drivers saying that they must not scramble their cars; they must all drive their cars in a sane, orderly fashion out of that lot.*

*Well, it was very interesting to see what happened. I felt the whole day was ruined when I envisioned eleven cars peeling out and forty-five other cars in single file paddling gently from the parking lot. But I explained the situation to the assistant director and he went around to get the Texans riled up by saying that Hollywood drivers were better than Texans. When the assistant director, Jim Fargo, waved the white flag, forty-eight of those fifty cars made dirt bike trails where none had been! And if you've seen the picture, it's one of the more spectacular scramble scenes in the movie.*

The Sugarland Express, which starred Goldie Hawn, made a major impression with movie critics. This film, like *Duel*, is filled with exciting car chases.

Of his next project, *Jaws*, Spielberg said he felt almost like he was "directing the audience with an electric cattle prod." The plot of *Jaws* is basically similar to that of *Duel*. In *Duel*, the cause of the terror is a monster truck; in *Jaws*, it is a monster shark. The drama in each case comes from how ordinary people respond to the deadly threat presented.

Although the rewards for making *Jaws* were enormous, the experience was not a happy one for cast or crew. The screenplay was rewritten at least five times. Spielberg continued to change the script even while he was shooting the movie.

Spielberg's trickiest task in *Jaws* was directing several mechanical sharks, all nicknamed "Bruce." Their frequent failures came close to killing the film.

To play the part of the great white shark, the special effects team built three large mechanical models (together nicknamed "Bruce" by the crew). One model swam from left to right; the second swam from right to left; and the third was for full-body shots underwater. Each model was operated electrically by remote control and could be moved by compressed air. The problem was that the mechanical sharks, which looked and tested fine on dry land, failed time and again when exposed to salt water. Bruce's costly failures almost torpedoed the film.

Shark hunters Richard Dreyfuss (left) and Robert Shaw brace themselves as "Bruce" prepares to attack.

The mechanical sharks worked so rarely that Spielberg often had to suggest the presence of the shark rather than show it. He was helped by the music that his friend John Williams wrote for the film. Two notes, repeated relentlessly, tell us the shark is near, even when we do not see it. Williams won an Oscar for the music for *Jaws*, and he won again for his music for *E.T. the Extra-Terrestrial*. He probably would have won for *Close Encounters of the Third Kind* if the Academy had not chosen an even greater Williams score from the same year—his music for *Star Wars*!

# CHAPTER 4

# EXPLORING NEW WORLDS

During the next decade and a half, Spielberg used the freedom he had earned through the success of *Jaws* to explore many different types of films. He made two science fiction classics, *Close Encounters of the Third Kind* (1977) and *E.T. the Extra-Terrestrial* (1982). He made three successful action-adventure yarns, *Raiders of the Lost Ark* (1981), *Indiana Jones and the Temple of Doom* (1984), and *Indiana Jones and the Last Crusade* (1989). He traveled to China to film *Empire of the Sun* (1987), an epic drama about a British boy imprisoned by the Japanese. He directed a comedy, *1941* (1979), and an old-fashioned romance, *Always* (1989)—both of which flopped with audiences and critics alike. He wrote the screenplay and played a behind-the-scenes role in making the horror film **Poltergeist** (1982). And he made the most hotly debated movie of his career, *The Color Purple* (1985), his first effort to portray the African-American experience.

As much of a **workaholic** as his father, Spielberg also took an active role as a producer. This was especially true after he set up Amblin Entertainment in 1984 with his coproducers, Frank Marshall and Kathleen Kennedy. In addition to producing many of his own films and the television series *Amazing Stories*, he also provided the backing for popular films by other directors.

In *E.T.*, Spielberg based the character of Elliott partly on his own boyhood. Here Elliott (played by Henry Thomas) pedals his bike as fast as he can to help E.T. get "home."

These included the *Back to the Future* series, the animated *An American Tail*, and the pioneering film *Who Framed Roger Rabbit*, which mixed human actors with cartoon characters.

## FRIENDLY ALIENS

*Close Encounters* and *E.T.* are two of Spielberg's most beloved films. They are also two of the most unusual movies in the history of science fiction. Space aliens have often been portrayed as threatening. In these two films, Spielberg deliberately avoided the kind of scare tactics he used in *Duel* and *Jaws*. In both *Close Encounters* and *E.T.*, the conflict in the film comes not from the aliens—who mean no harm to anyone—but from the different ways that people view the visitors from space.

For the first time since his student days, Spielberg wrote his own original screenplay for *Close Encounters*. (The plot is similar in some ways to his Phoenix feature, *Firelight*.) Like much of his work, it draws heavily on his memories of when he was growing up, such as the memory of his father waking him up in the middle of the night to view a meteor shower. He also remembered the rumors about UFOs, or unidentified flying objects— what people called "flying saucers."

A key to his imagination was the song "When You Wish Upon a Star," from the Walt Disney movie *Pinocchio*. As in the Disney film, music plays a major role in *Close Encounters*. The aliens do not use words to communicate with people. They speak through a symphony of sound and light, as composed by John

Before Spielberg, the most popular American filmmaker was probably Walt Disney. "When You Wish Upon a Star," a beloved song from Disney's animated film *Pinocchio*, inspired Spielberg when he was making *Close Encounters of the Third Kind*.

# Film Focus: Working with Children

In a famous scene from *Close Encounters*, Cary Guffey stands before an open doorway, bathed in light. How did Spielberg get a quality performance from the very young actor?

*I had to the left of the camera a cardboard partition, and to the right of the camera a second cardboard partition. To the left of the camera, I put Bob Westmoreland, our makeup man, in a gorilla suit—the full mask and hands and hairy body. To the right of the camera, I dressed myself up as an Easter Bunny, with the ears and the nose and the whiskers painted on my face. Cary Guffey didn't know what to expect. He didn't know what he was gonna react to. His job was to come into the kitchen, stop at the door, and just have a good time. . . . Just as he came into the kitchen, I had the cardboard partition dropped and Bob Westmoreland was there as the gorilla. Cary froze, like a deer caught in car headlights. . . . I dropped my partition, and he looked over at me, and there was the Easter Bunny smiling at him. He was torn. He began to smile at me—he was still afraid of that thing. Then I had Bob—I said, "Take off your head." Bob took off his mask, and when Cary saw it was the man that put his makeup on in the morning, Cary began to laugh. Even though it was a trick, the reaction was pure and honest.*

Williams and filmed by the Oscar-winning cinematographer Vilmos Zsigmond.

When making films like *Close Encounters*, Spielberg incorporated influences he received from other directors and films, including Stanley Kubrick and the science fiction film *2001*.

Another filmmaker he much admired (and who, like Spielberg, has often been praised for his wonderful way of working with children) was the French director François Truffaut. Spielberg showed his respect for Truffaut by giving the Frenchman a role in his film as a well-meaning scientist. Truffaut offered this portrait of Spielberg on the set: "He really isn't pretentious, he doesn't behave like the director of the most successful film in the history of the cinema . . . he's calm (outwardly so), very even-tempered, very patient and good-humored. This film of flying saucers means a great deal to him, it's a childhood dream come true."

The French film director François Truffaut (right) made a rare appearance as an actor in *Close Encounters,* playing the role of a sensitive scientist.

Five years after filming *Close Encounters,* Spielberg returned to the space alien theme in *E.T. the Extra-Terrestrial,* which was originally titled *E.T. and Me*—a sign that this movie was very close to the director's heart. While *Close Encounters* has lots of special effects, some parts of *E.T.* feel very low-tech. Even the device that the space creature uses to "phone home" is made from a Speak 'n' Spell toy and other household items.

*E.T.* is a story about loneliness and love. It is no secret that Spielberg based the character of Elliott partly on his own boyhood. As the movie begins, Elliott's father has moved out of the house—just as Spielberg's dad did when he was growing up. There is also something very childlike about E.T., who shares Elliott's loneliness because he was left behind when his fellow creatures departed. When E.T. falls ill, modern medicine cannot save him, but Elliott's love does.

Today, many critics regard *E.T.* as Spielberg's most nearly perfect film. "*E.T.* is the teddy bear we crush

One of the many ways Spielberg shows the deep bond between E.T. and Elliott is through their names: E and T are the first and last letters of Elliott's name.

A huge rolling boulder is only one of the many perils Harrison Ford had to survive as Indiana Jones in *Raiders of the Lost Ark.*

Before she married Spielberg, Kate Capshaw (right) co-starred as Willie Scott in *Indiana Jones and the Temple of Doom.*

forever to our bleeding hearts," wrote Andrew Sarris. "*E.T.* is every childish fantasy we never outgrew. *E.T.* is the eternal child in all of us." The film was an instant hit, attracting over $400 million in U.S. box-office revenues when it was released in 1982 and re-released twenty years later. It was Spielberg's biggest box-office success until surpassed by *Jurassic Park* in 1993.

## GREAT ESCAPES

In between *Close Encounters* and *E.T.*, Spielberg directed *Raiders of the Lost Ark*, the first film in what has become known as the Indiana Jones **trilogy**. (A fourth movie in the series is planned, possibly for as early as 2004.) Spielberg developed *Raiders* with George Lucas, the creator of *Star Wars* (1977).

The two men shared a fondness for the action-packed **serials** of the 1930s and 1940s. These films were called serials because, like television series today, they were meant to be seen weekly. Typically, movie theaters would show a new episode each Saturday. At the end of one episode, the hero might be left hanging by his fingernails on the edge of a cliff; to find out how he escapes, the audience would have to come back the next week. This is the origin of the term cliffhanger, which describes a particular kind of suspense film. Lucas and Spielberg wanted to make old-time cliffhangers, only with much better writing, acting, and special effects.

In fact, *Raiders* and its two sequels, *Indiana Jones and the Temple of Doom* (1984) and *Indiana Jones and the Last Crusade* (1989), share many features with *Star Wars* and its 1980s sequels, *The Empire Strikes Back* (1980) and *Return of the Jedi* (1983). The actor who plays Indiana Jones is Harrison Ford, who first became famous as Han Solo in *Star Wars*. Writer-director Lawrence Kasdan had a hand in the scripts for *Raiders*, *Empire*, and *Jedi*. John Williams composed the music for all six films.

The basic formula for the three Indiana Jones films is the same. In each movie, Indy—an **archaeologist** and adventurer—and a large cast of good and bad characters set out to find some object with mysterious powers. In *Temple of Doom*, which takes place mostly in India, the villains are members of a bloody religious cult; in the first and third films, the chief evildoers are the Nazis in World War II. Each Indiana Jones movie has all the bumps and thrills of a great roller coaster ride—and about as much depth, some people complained.

## Film Focus: Storyboarding

Many filmmakers begin a movie by storyboarding. They lay out the film scene by scene, shot by shot, with a series of rough sketches, called storyboards. They then "shoot the paper"—in other words, they treat the storyboards as their road map for shooting the movie. This technique works for many films but not all of them, as Spielberg noted in 1982.

*All of my movies prior to* E.T. *were storyboarded. I designed the picture visually on paper and then shot the paper, embellishing things as I went along, because a piece of paper with a one-dimensional sketch is only a starting-point. You have to breathe life into that sketch through characterization, atmosphere, movement, sound, and all sorts of things. I'd always designed my movies on paper . . . [until] I decided I was tired of spending two months with a piece of paper and a pencil and a couple of sketch artists interpreting my stick figures. I decided to wing* E.T. *Winging* E.T. *made it a very spontaneous, vital movie. Not that the other ones aren't, but I surprised myself. I realized I didn't need the drawings for a small movie like* E.T. *. . . . It was much better to start with personalities and let the personalities suggest where the camera goes as opposed to setting the camera in cement and instructing an actor where to sit, stand, and move because that's what the little doodles suggested.*

Harrison Ford (left) appeared as Indiana Jones for a third time in *Indiana Jones and the Last Crusade,* which featured Sean Connery (right) as Indy's dad.

Yet another Spielberg movie with a World War II setting was *Empire of the Sun.* Views were divided about this beautifully photographed film, which tells the story of a boy who is separated from his parents and comes of age in a Japanese prison camp. For the most part, audiences stayed away. Box office receipts were less than $70 million worldwide—not bad for most directors, but a failure by Steven Spielberg standards.

## Film Focus: Special Effects

Filmgoers expect to see great special effects in a Steven Spielberg movie: a monster shark chomping a boat, dinosaurs running amok, E.T. and Elliott soaring skyward on a bike. But the director insists that the special effects should serve the story, and not the other way around.

*Using special effects is only another way around something that can't be created naturally. A special effect is an alternative to making a direct deal with God and asking Him to part the Red Sea or create a fantastic light-show in the sky or allow us to see spirits of the past floating through space. . . . Failing that, you need special effects. I find the most successful special effects are when it appears that you did make some sort of "special arrangement [with God]." The worst special effects to me are the kind that cause the audience to say, "Look at that great effect." The best special effects cause the audience to truly suspend their disbelief and watch wonders unfold before them.*

## BLACK AND WHITE AND THE COLOR PURPLE

*The Color Purple* holds a special place among Spielberg's movies of the 1980s. The film, based on a prize-winning novel by Alice Walker, stars Whoopi Goldberg as Celie, a young woman who is abused by her father, mistreated by her husband, and cruelly separated from her sister. Although Celie's life is very hard, she eventually finds pride, strength, and love. In a very emotional scene at the end of the film, she and her sister are reunited.

Family, love, the triumph of good over evil: These sound like the usual Spielberg themes, but there are twists. All the major characters are black, the story is often grim, and when the grown-up Celie first finds love, she finds it in the arms of a woman. Many thought *The Color Purple* was an odd movie for a white male to direct—especially since Spielberg was known for making films based on fantastic stories, not serious novels.

Spielberg, a target of prejudice as a teenager, felt deep sympathy with Celie, but he, too, had doubts about whether he should direct the film. "Don't you want to find a black director or a woman?" he asked Quincy Jones, an African-American composer and musician who coproduced and wrote the music for the movie. "You didn't have to come from Mars to do *E.T.*, did you?" answered Jones.

Spielberg was right to be worried. Both the movie and the book were criticized for making African-American men look bad. Some critics complained that the film's rich colors seemed at odds with the stark truth of black poverty in the South between 1900 and 1950.

On the other hand, *The Color Purple* was a surprise hit with audiences, bringing in more than $140 million worldwide. It made a sincere attempt to show the African-American experience at a time when few Hollywood movies bothered to try. It also gave a tremendous boost to the careers of two gifted performers, Whoopi Goldberg and Oprah Winfrey, who had their first major roles on the big screen in this film.

Whoopi Goldberg made her feature-film debut playing Celie in *The Color Purple*. Her starring performance earned her an Oscar nomination; she later won an Academy Award for her supporting role in *Ghost* (1990).

# CHAPTER 5

# PETER PAN GROWS UP

Spielberg and Amy Irving were a glamorous twosome at a Los Angeles film festival in 1977. They married in 1985 and divorced four years later.

The director enjoys a family outing with his second wife, Kate Capshaw.

Spielberg found himself at a crossroads at the end of the 1980s. Partly, the reason was personal. In June 1985, his longtime companion, actress Amy Irving, had given birth to their son, Max. By coincidence, Irving went into labor just as Spielberg was directing a highly dramatic childbirth scene in *The Color Purple*. "Honey," she told him, "now come and direct my delivery." Five months later, they were married.

The marriage did not last long. Like his father, Spielberg found it difficult to balance the demands of career and home life. Matters were complicated by the fact that Irving also had an acting career and did not want to stand in her famous husband's shadow. In 1989, they let the world know they were splitting up.

By this time, Spielberg was already involved with another actress, Kate Capshaw. The director first met her when she tried out for the part of Willie Scott in *Indiana Jones and the Temple of Doom*. She found the relationship with Spielberg much more rewarding than the role, which, among other things, required her to let bugs crawl all over her body. While playing Willie, she said, "I felt that some days all I did was shriek, and it was exhausting."

In May 1990, she gave birth to their first child, a girl named Sasha. They were married a year and a half later, after she had converted to Judaism. By the end of the decade, several more youngsters were growing up in their household, including two African-American children whom they had adopted. Like Spielberg, Capshaw also has a child from a previous marriage.

With his home life more stable, Spielberg began to rethink what he wanted to do as a filmmaker. As the 1990s began, he was in his mid-forties. He had made some of the most exciting and entertaining movies in Hollywood history. He was wealthy. But he had never made a fully mature movie for grown-ups, about grown-ups, that had succeeded in winning praise from both audiences and critics.

Some writers had a name for his problem. They called it the **Peter Pan syndrome**. In the children's book by James M. Barrie (which Leah Spielberg often read to her young son at bedtime), Peter Pan wants to stay a little boy forever. Spielberg recognized the issue in 1985 when he said, "I have always felt like Peter Pan. I still feel like Peter Pan. It has been very hard for me to grow up."

## Film Focus: Test Screenings

Before a film is released, it is usually previewed by test audiences. If an audience does not respond well, some scenes might be changed, or a new ending might be written. At one time, Spielberg liked previews. Here is what he said in 1982:

*After this extraordinary preview in Dallas of* Jaws, *I still didn't feel I had a big enough reaction in the second act of the movie, so I designed the head coming out of the hole in the boat, which I shot in a friend's swimming pool. And that became the big scream of the movie. I felt the movie needed an explosive surprise at that point. The preview helped to expose a weakness so I could fill the gap.*

A decade and a half later, however, the mature filmmaker took a much more negative view of test screenings.

*The movies that I personally direct I don't test. I haven't tested a movie since* Hook *in 1991. I think tests are deceiving. Even though the critical community . . . trounced that film, the test scores were some of the highest that had ever been gotten by a movie. People who got in to see* Hook *for free, in the one test screening, liked the movie a hell of a lot better than people who wound up having to pay for it and didn't think it was worth five or six bucks.*

Spielberg was in his mid-forties when he made *Hook,* his attempt to come to terms with the "Peter Pan syndrome." Above: Robin Williams as Peter Pan (left) crosses swords with Dustin Hoffman as Captain Hook. Below: Hoffman discusses a scene with Spielberg.

Spielberg tried to confront the problem in *Hook* (1991), his own version of the Peter Pan story. This is one of the director's very few movies to feature a big-name cast: Robin Williams as the grown-up Peter, Dustin Hoffman as Captain Hook, and Julia Roberts as Tinkerbell. Star power helped ensure strong ticket sales, but the critics were merciless in calling the film an artistic failure.

TIME TO GROW UP

Was Hollywood's own Peter Pan really ready to grow up? Audiences got another clue in the summer of 1993—and the answer was, not yet. Like many people, Spielberg had been fascinated by dinosaurs when he was a kid. Unlike just about anyone else, however, he was able to hire the best technical wizards in the business, make use of the latest and hottest computer graphics, and create *Jurassic Park.* Experts quibbled about the science

Velociraptors stalk their human prey in the pulse-pounding climax to *Jurassic Park*.

behind the movie, and critics complained about the script. But audiences were stunned by how real the dinosaurs looked. The movie broke U.S. box-office records and earned more than $900 million worldwide.

## Film Focus: Computer Graphics

Many of the dinosaur effects in *Jurassic Park* and *The Lost World: Jurassic Park 2* were created by computer. Computer graphics imaging, or CGI, can be incredibly realistic, but top-quality CGI still comes at a very steep price, as Spielberg told a reporter in 1997.

*It still runs you between $250,000 and $500,000 to put anything into a computer, even a small, uncomplicated dinosaur, and that's before you generate a single shot. If you've got a dinosaur just walking around, it's $60,000 for eight seconds. If the dinosaur is splashing in a puddle or kicking up tufts of dirt, it's $100,000. If there are four dinosaurs in the background of that shot, it's $150,000.*

*The Lost World: Jurassic Park 2* relied on large robots and computer graphics to create real-looking dinosaurs like this stegosaurus.

*Jurassic Park* raked in so much money that Spielberg could not resist making a sequel, *The Lost World: Jurassic Park 2* (1997), which was also a smash.

Spielberg addressed the concerns of the critics in December 1993 with the release of *Schindler's List*. The subject of the film is one of history's most monstrous crimes—the **Holocaust**, the slaughter of millions of European Jews and others during World War II.

The director had been thinking of making a film about the Holocaust for a long time. While growing up, he had heard about family members killed by the Nazis. "The Holocaust had been part of my life, just based on what my parents would say at the dinner table," Spielberg recalled in 1993. "We lost cousins, aunts, uncles. When I was very young, I remember my mother telling me about a friend of hers in Germany, a pianist. . . . The Germans came up on stage and broke every finger on her hands. I grew up with stories of Nazis breaking the fingers of Jews."

*Schindler* is a Holocaust movie, but it is also a Spielberg movie. In making *Schindler*, the director chose a true story that offered a few rays of hope in a very dark time. The plot, based on a novel by Thomas Keneally, revolves around Oskar Schindler, a Christian businessman who is also a Nazi. At first, Schindler's only interest in the Jews is as a source of cheap labor for his factory. As time goes on, however, he takes more and more risks in order to save the Jews from death. As many as

In making a movie about the Holocaust, Spielberg chose a story about a German Christian businessman who offered Jews a helping hand.

These young people were among the few who survived the Nazi death camp at Auschwitz.

twelve hundred Jews who survived the Holocaust owed their lives to Oskar Schindler's efforts.

Spielberg avoided many of the problems that had plagued him on *The Color Purple*. The Jewish struggle was a subject he knew and felt from the inside, not one he had learned about secondhand. Nearly the whole film was shot in black and white, which gave *Schindler's List* a stark look that matched the seriousness of its subject. He started with a first-rate script by Steven Zaillian and added superb cinematography by Janusz Kaminski. The film won the Academy Award for Best Picture and six other Oscars. These included individual honors for Spielberg, Zaillian, Kaminski, and John Williams, who wrote one of his most moving musical scores.

## SHOWMAN WITH A CONSCIENCE

Spielberg rode a wave of popular and critical approval into the mid-1990s. He used a generous share of the profits from *Schindler's List* to establish the Survivors of

At the heart of *Schindler's List* is the relationship between Oskar Schindler, a Christian businessman played by Liam Neeson (left), and Itzhak Stern, a Jewish accountant portrayed by Ben Kingsley.

Spielberg and his mother share the glow on Oscar night.

Actress Helen Hunt (left) and Spielberg stand with a Holocaust survivor at a Shoah Foundation event in 2001.

Spielberg was awarded the National Humanities Medal in 1999 by President Bill Clinton and First Lady Hillary Rodham Clinton.

the **Shoah** Visual History Foundation. (Shoah is the Hebrew word for the Holocaust.) The purpose of the Shoah Foundation is to videotape and preserve the stories of Holocaust survivors. The Foundation has collected statements from more than 50,000 eyewitnesses in dozens of countries.

Spielberg, a Democrat, also became more active in politics. He was one of the film world's leading supporters of Bill Clinton, a Democrat who was elected president of the United States in 1992 and again in 1996.

During the same period, the director was a major player in one of Hollywood's biggest business deals. In 1994, Spielberg cofounded DreamWorks SKG with Jeffrey Katzenberg and David Geffen. (The initials "SKG" stand for the first letter of each man's last name.) DreamWorks has become one of the nation's most important entertainment companies, producing television shows, music recordings, videos, DVDs, and such hit movies as *Chicken Run*, *Gladiator*, and *Shrek*.

## D-DAY AND BEYOND

Spielberg has continued to explore familiar themes in his most recent movies, also made for DreamWorks. His most acclaimed work of the late 1990s was *Saving Private Ryan* (1998), starring Tom Hanks. He intended *Ryan* as a tribute to the generation of men who, like his father, had fought in World War II.

The most remarkable footage comes early in the film.

It is a re-creation of the D-Day invasion—the battle that began on the beaches of northern France on June 6, 1944, when Allied troops began to reclaim Europe from the Nazis. The young Spielberg would have planned out every moment of the entire scene on storyboards. The mature director let the camera roam freely across the battlefield, showing the chaos and confusion of war. Special types of films and camera filters, plus terrifying sound effects, also convey an eerie sense of being an actual part of the battle.

Many people who were veterans of World War II (and many people who were not) were moved to tears by the film. Spielberg earned an Oscar for directing *Saving Private Ryan*, and he also was given a Distinguished Public Service Award from the U.S. Department of Defense. He continued to honor the heroes of World War II with the cable television series *Band of*

*Saving Private Ryan* earned Spielberg his second Oscar as best director.

The D-Day invasion in *Saving Private Ryan* is one of the grimmest and most realistic battle scenes ever filmed.

In *Amistad,* as in *Schindler,* Spielberg tried to tell an uplifting story about an ugly period in human history. *Amistad* shows how a group of African men rebelled against slavery and eventually won their freedom.

Spielberg made *A.I.* (below) as a tribute to director Stanley Kubrick (bottom right). Kubrick's science fiction film *2001* had a potent influence on many directors, including Spielberg and George Lucas.

*Brothers* (2001), which he coproduced with Hanks.

Two other recent films were less well received. Spielberg revisited African-American history in *Amistad* (1997), which told the true story of a slave rebellion and court case in 1839–1841. The film was well meaning, and this time few people questioned his right to make it. But audiences stayed away, and some reviewers complained that the film felt more like a history lesson than a real-life human drama.

*A.I.* (2001) is Spielberg's tribute to director Stanley Kubrick, who first developed the idea for the movie but died before he could make the film. *A.I.*—the full title is *A.I. Artificial Intelligence*—portrays a robot, played by Haley Joel Osment, who wants to be a real boy. Some writers thought the movie was a deep exploration of what it means to be fully human. Others thought this retelling of the Pinocchio story was hurt by a clash between Spielberg's warmhearted style and Kubrick's icy approach.

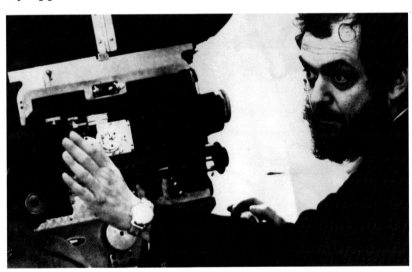

As Spielberg reached and passed his fiftieth birthday, the honors that had eluded him in earlier decades began to stack up. In addition to his Oscars, he received life achievement awards from the American Film Institute in 1995 and the Directors Guild of America five years later. In 2001, he was dubbed Knight of the British Empire by Queen Elizabeth II of England.

Spielberg appears healthy, vigorous, and—by current standards—relatively young. He could easily be making movies for another ten or twenty years or more. "I have made a lot of the films that I wanted to make over the last 25 years," he told the *New York Times* in 2001. "But the thing that I've allowed myself is to let time change my mind about the kind of films I always thought I wanted to make. I've left myself open to how my tastes have changed with my ever-changing life."

## TV Programs Directed by Spielberg

*Night Gallery* ("Eyes," 1969; "Make Me Laugh," 1971)

*Marcus Welby, M.D.* ("The Daredevil Gesture," 1970)

*The Name of the Game* ("L.A. 2017," 1971)

*The Psychiatrist* ("The Private World of Martin Dalton," 1971; "Par for the Course," 1971)

*Columbo* ("Murder by the Book," 1971)

*Owen Marshall, Counselor at Law* ("Eulogy for a Wide Receiver," 1971)

*Duel* (1971; also released in theaters)

*Something Evil* (1972)

*Savage* (1973)

*Amazing Stories* ("Ghost Train," 1985; "The Mission," 1987)

Listed in the order they were broadcast.

Spielberg still loves working behind a movie camera, as shown in this photo from the set of *Indiana Jones and the Temple of Doom*.

# Spielberg Blockbusters

One way of measuring a movie's success is by the box-office gross—how much money people paid to see the film in theaters. Of the one hundred top-grossing films of all time, Spielberg directed eleven, more than any other director. The following list of estimated box-office receipts was compiled in early 2002, before the re-release of *E.T.*

| Film | Box-Office Receipts (in millions) | | | All-time rank |
| --- | --- | --- | --- | --- |
| | U.S. | Foreign | Total | |
| *Jurassic Park* (1993) | $357.1 | $563.0 | $920.1 | 4 |
| *E.T.* (1982) | $399.8 | $301.0 | $700.8 | 9 |
| *The Lost World: Jurassic Park 2* (1997) | $229.1 | $385.0 | $614.1 | 12 |
| *Indiana Jones and the Last Crusade* (1989) | $197.2 | $297.6 | $494.8 | 22 |
| *Saving Private Ryan* (1998) | $215.9 | $256.8 | $472.7 | 25 |
| *Jaws* (1975) | $260.0 | $210.6 | $470.6 | 26 |
| *Raiders of the Lost Ark* (1981) | $242.4 | $141.5 | $383.9 | 47 |
| *Close Encounters of the Third Kind* (1977) | $166.0 | $171.7 | $337.7 | 73 |
| *Indiana Jones and the Temple of Doom* (1984) | $179.9 | $153.2 | $333.1 | 76 |
| *Schindler's List* (1993) | $96.1 | $221.0 | $317.1 | 88 |
| *Hook* (1991) | $119.7 | $181.2 | $300.9 | 96 |

Source: The Movie Times web site (www.the-movie-times.com)

# Filmography:
## Feature Films Directed by Spielberg

*The Sugarland Express* (1974)

*Jaws* (1975)

*Close Encounters of the Third Kind* (1977)

*1941* (1979)

*Raiders of the Lost Ark* (1981)

*E.T. the Extra-Terrestrial* (1982)

*Indiana Jones and the Temple of Doom* (1984)

*The Color Purple* (1985)

*Empire of the Sun* (1987)

*Indiana Jones and the Last Crusade* (1989)

*Always* (1989)

*Hook* (1991)

*Jurassic Park* (1993)

*Schindler's List* (1993)

*The Lost World: Jurassic Park 2* (1997)

*Amistad* (1997)

*Saving Private Ryan* (1998)

*A.I.* (2001)

*Minority Report* (2002)

Listed in order of theatrical release.

Like any great director, Spielberg has a clear vision of each film he wants to make, whether he's shooting a high-tech blockbuster like *Jurassic Park* (below) or an old-fashioned romance like *Always* (bottom left).

| 1946 | Steven Allan Spielberg is born December 18, in Cincinnati, Ohio |
| 1949 | Moves to New Jersey. |
| 1957 | Moves to Arizona; as a boy, directs his first movie, *The Last Train Wreck* |
| 1964 | Moves to California; attends California State College at Long Beach |
| 1968 | Directs *Amblin'*; lands a contract with Universal Studios |
| 1969 | Directs Hollywood legend Joan Crawford in *Night Gallery* |
| 1971 | *Duel* airs as a made-for-TV movie on ABC |
| 1974 | *The Sugarland Express* earns rave reviews from critics |
| 1975 | *Jaws*, the first Hollywood blockbuster, opens on June 20 |
| 1977 | *Close Encounters of the Third Kind* is released |
| 1981 | *Raiders of the Lost Ark* is released; sequels follow in 1984 and 1989 |
| 1985 | Marries Amy Irving (they divorce in 1989) |
| 1986 | *The Color Purple* (1985) is nominated for eleven Academy Awards but wins none |
| 1987 | Wins his first Oscar—the honorary Irving G. Thalberg Memorial Award |
| 1991 | Marries Kate Capshaw |
| 1993 | *Jurassic Park* and *Schindler's List* are released |
| 1994 | *Schindler's List* earns the Academy Award as Best Picture; earns first Oscar for directing; DreamWorks SKG is founded; establishes the Survivors of the Shoah Visual History Foundation |
| 1995 | Receives the American Film Institute Life Achievement Award |
| 1997 | *The Lost World: Jurassic Park 2* and *Amistad* are released |
| 1999 | Earns second directing Oscar for *Saving Private Ryan* (1998) |
| 2000 | Receives Lifetime Achievement Award from the Directors Guild of America |
| 2001 | Receives honorary knighthood from Queen Elizabeth II of England; *Band of Brothers* airs on HBO; *A.I.* is released |
| 2002 | Receives bachelor of arts degree after completing requirements he left unfinished when he dropped out of college in 1968. |

**Academy Awards:** the highest honors in the movie industry; the Academy Awards, also known as Oscars, are presented each year by the Academy of Motion Picture Arts and Sciences

**affluent:** wealthy

**archaeologist:** someone who looks for and studies objects from the ancient past

**cinematographer:** in feature films, the person directly in charge of how a scene is lit and shot

**debut:** first appearance

**dialogue:** a discussion involving two or more people

**directors:** people in charge of all the creative aspects of making a film or television program

**filmography:** a list of films

**Holocaust:** the murder of millions of Jews and others during World War II

**Nazis:** members of a political party that controlled Germany from 1933 to 1945

**Oscars:** *see* Academy Awards

**Peter Pan syndrome:** term applied to an adult who refuses to grow up

**poltergeist:** a mischievous ghost

**producer:** the person in charge of all the business aspects of making a film or television program

**serials:** in the 1930s and 1940s, short action films that were meant to be seen weekly, usually on Saturday mornings

**Shoah:** Hebrew word for the Holocaust

**studio:** a large television or movie production company; also, the place where the film or video is shot

**trilogy:** a series of three related films

**workaholic:** someone who works very long hours

**World War II:** world conflict fought between 1939 and 1945; the Allies (including the United States, the Soviet Union, Britain, and France) defeated the Axis powers (including Germany, Italy, and Japan)

# TO FIND OUT MORE

## BOOKS

Brode, Douglas. *The Films of Steven Spielberg*. New York: Citadel Press, 2000 (rev. ed.).

Craddock, Jim (ed.). *VideoHound's Golden Movie Retriever 2002*. Farmington Hills, Mich.: Gale Group, 2001.

Friedman, Lester D., and Brent Notbohm. *Steven Spielberg: Interviews*. Jackson, Miss.: University Press of Mississippi, 2000.

Gottfried, Ted. *Steven Spielberg: From Reels to Riches*. New York: Franklin Watts, 2000.

Powers, Tom. *Steven Spielberg*. Minneapolis: Lerner Publications, 2000.

Rubin, Susan Goldman. *Steven Spielberg: Crazy for Movies*. New York: Harry N. Abrams, 2001.

## INTERNET SITES

### Academy of Motion Picture Arts and Sciences

*www.oscars.org*

AMPAS is the organization that hands out the annual Academy Awards, or Oscars.

### DreamWorks SKG

*www.dreamworks.com*

Official site of the entertainment company Spielberg cofounded in 1994.

### Steven Spielberg Jewish Film Archive

*sites.huji.ac.il/jfa/jfa.htm*

A collection of more than three thousand documentary films and videos located in Israel.

### Survivors of the Shoah Visual History Foundation

*www.vhf.org*

Web site of the group founded by Spielberg after he made *Schindler's List*.

# INDEX *(continued)*

## About the Author

**Geoffrey M. Horn** is a freelance writer and editor with a lifelong interest in politics and the arts. He is the author of books for young people and adults and has contributed hundreds of articles to encyclopedias and other reference books, including *The World Almanac*. He graduated summa cum laude with a bachelor's degree in English literature from Columbia University, in New York City, and holds a master's degree with honors from St. John's College, Cambridge, England. He lives in southwestern Virginia in the foothills of the Blue Ridge Mountains. He dedicates this book to Marcia, his wife and favorite moviegoing companion for more than thirty-five years.